Miracle
Awakening

Miracle Awakening

What Will the Future Be Like?
What Will Your Future Be?

Kenneth Foley

WESTBOW
PRESS®
A DIVISION OF THOMAS NELSON
& ZONDERVAN

KJV: Scripture taken from King James Version of the Bible.

WestBow Press books may be ordered through booksellers or by contacting:

WestBow Press
A Division of Thomas Nelson & Zondervan
1663 Liberty Drive
Bloomington, IN 47403
www.westbowpress.com
1 (866) 928-1240

ISBN: 978-1-5127-9120-4 (sc)
ISBN: 978-1-5127-9119-8 (hc)
ISBN: 978-1-5127-9121-1 (e)

Library of Congress Control Number: 2017909614

Print information available on the last page.

WestBow Press rev. date: 06/26/2017

Contents

Has the Sunrise of Miracles Begun?

Chapter 1

Are the Heavens About to Open?

When you look up to the sky, what do you see? Can you see God? Do you see the heavens he made? Do you wonder where we fit in the heavens? Do you wonder how a planet so small in such a remote part of the universe became an intelligent, thriving planet when as far as we can see in the heavens there's no planet like ours?

Do you wonder what is about to happen to humankind on this tiny planet? Have we run out of room, or have we run out of ideas? Will the future be one great disaster after another as so many have told us, or are we about to see the heavens open to us in a way no civilization has seen before?

What do you see in the future? Are you convinced there is no hope and we are doomed by our evil? Do we deserve to be given a great disaster? Will we at last learn its lesson?

What if the opposite is true and we are about to receive the greatest influx of miracles humankind has ever seen? What if it has already begun to happen? What if doomsayers and false prophets are wrong and the opposite is true?

What would you say if we found out the sun was not setting on humankind but just beginning to rise? What would change in your life if you discovered we are beginning to see more miracles of God than we have ever seen? What if they are wonderful and beautiful beyond belief?

These are all interesting questions, but when the fog lifts from our minds' eyes, what will we see? It's as if the curtain is about to go up in the theater and we're trying to find our seats and get comfortable with our popcorn and drink. Should we expect the greatest show ever to begin because God deemed it so?

Why is there so much anticipation about what's about to happen? Are we so curious about it that we cannot wait for it to begin? Have we at last awakened the God of the heavens and now at long last he's going to show us the next act or next scene? Are we expecting something big and disastrous to happen in the next few years, months, or even days? Are we in a frenzied state of anticipation? Are we waiting for something to happen because we are now so intelligent and we seek answers everywhere? We want answers, and we want them now.

God, you are supposed to be a God of love, so show us answers and we'll believe you love us. We're your children; we don't want a stone, we want a loaf of hot, fresh bread with lots of butter. We want it now or we'll act sinfully bad some more and you'll be sorry, God who made us.

Is that where we are? Is this the way we want to play the game with a powerful God? Are we certain that if we're evil enough, God will send down more fire and brimstone? Are we daring God to reprimand us? Are we having a temper tantrum of biblical proportions that echoes into the heavens so loudly that God will cover his ears and finally say "Enough"?

Are we shaking our fists in God's face, defying his creation, and belittling all he made by saying it would have happened anyway in spite of the fact we don't know why the universe came about with its complicated and delicately balanced systems?

Are we saying some ancient aliens created it all long before we existed and will be back soon and it'll be all right? Whatever our semi-educated guesses are, should we simply throw out the possibility God exists? There's a small chance he does exist, so why not try seeking him the old-fashioned way—through prayer? What if we prayed and God answered? What if we prayed for a miracle and God performed it? Would we then believe God existed, or would we require a few more miracles?

What would it take to believe God exists? Is it even remotely possible that everyone would believe under any circumstances? Then again, maybe you already believe and have prayed and experienced miracles. No matter where you stand with God, believer and unbeliever alike, read on and see if you believe more in God after reading this book.

For the many millions who believe he exists, life is simple; they simply pray. They believe God hears and answers prayers, yet many millions of others stumble through dirt pile after dirt pile to find a clue that he doesn't exist. We use huge telescopes and technology to provide a simple explanation of life. We come and go as civilizations, one greater or lesser than the other. But what difference does that make? We want to say that there's a natural explanation for anything that happens and that's all we need.

Didn't cave people carve images on the walls, and didn't other ancient civilizations believe in God? Where did that get any of them? They're dead. So much for a living God who lets us die. Unless the one true God did something different and gave us life after death. That seems to be the basis of most religions, but how do we prove that?

Our reasoning is upside down. We search the heavens with telescopes only to find one more reason after another that proves it couldn't be one more simple thing that caused it all to come into existence. Even microscopes can't find where it all began. It's almost like God keeps scientists mystified while he laughs at their futile efforts. Are we like children who can't believe our parents know so much and we know so little? How much more humiliation do we need before we say, "All right! I give up. There must be an intelligent being who did all this. Let's call him God. Sounds like a good name to me. Oh, wait. People already call him God. Let give him a personal name. How about Jehovah? No, that's too Jewish. We need to be politically correct. Maybe we should just give him a number just like we do stars." We want science to feel right when we name someone or something. We want science to tell us there is a God.

Are we so ignorant that we prove things that do exist actually don't exist? When we need God, he suddenly exists, but when we don't need him—poof—he doesn't exist. That's the way some people believe in God. What if the same God who made us gave us rules to live by? Let's call those rules the Ten Commandments or the Golden Rule—to love one another. That's what Jesus taught us. But Jesus was not a modern, scientific chemical engineer. Or was he? He turned water into wine; that's called alchemy. He walked on water; that's not even in the Olympics. We cannot deny Jesus existed. He performed miracles beyond our comprehension. But people say, "Yes, but we can't find his remains. That's a problem. We need to put him in a museum. Okay, start looking for the body, somebody!"

I'm not sorry to inform those people that Jesus's body rose into the heavens after it arose from the grave. This defies all logic and is difficult to prove. Unless aliens caught him up into the air. But strangely, they haven't contacted us and taken credit for that feat. This may seem a little ridiculous, but how much different is this from the attempts science makes to discover truths and is totally frustrated by the missing evidence? The truth is that it's right there in plain sight. Or was until Jesus left and went to heaven.

The heavens seem to be opening as we start an era of travel to distant places. If we are about to discover something big, what will it be? What will we see or hear? Are we listening and looking to the sky because we hope something so grand happens that proves we can do what we'd only imagined? Now can we stand up after all the centuries of struggling to rise above something? But what do we want to rise above? Are we certain we have the strength to rise, or do we believe we've arrived and now is the moment of triumph? What will we rise above into? We haven't figured out how to get along here on earth and now we want to extend ourselves into the heavens? Perhaps it's only a business venture and we'll benefit from its technology. But let's continue and assume God will help us get it right.

Chapter 2

Is the Curtain Going Up or Coming Down?

Is the mystery of the future killing us? Are we sure we're unique in the heavens? Are we sure we're not like any other species? Are we certain we can perform unbelievable feats? Is our imagination running faster than we can think and reason? What's slowing us down? Why doesn't the curtain go up? Why can't we see the future? Isn't our future right in front of us? What if we find some form of life on another planet or on one of Saturn's moons? Would that mean God doesn't exist? Or would it prove only that his creation is everywhere—on earth but also in the heavens?

We wait day after day hoping for some sign of the future, and then an invention comes along. We call it a cell phone; we can speak to anyone anywhere. And driverless cars make their advent. Is the future already a part of us and we no longer have to wait for it to begin? Maybe God is hiding in our technology. Maybe he wants us to have cell phones and technology so we can enjoy life more than before. God may allow us to peek inside other planets and their moons in our solar system. God may be full of mind-boggling surprises.

Perhaps someone or something is controlling the world. Almost every civilization has had religious beliefs. Are we so advanced that we are looking backward and forward to verify everything and we're ending up confused about all creation? Has science and technology created within us a way to verify everything but we try to apply it to too many things in life? Are we looking at life through a microscope and losing the bigger picture?

The simplest truth is usually the best truth. We may be hoping for a certain outcome so much that we skew our data and believe we're correct no matter what we discover.

Can you imagine such a being existing beyond what we say can be imagined? What if it's possible for that being to exist and control your future and all he asks is that you make your request known to him in what is called a prayer?

Is it possible to utter a prayer with our minds?

Chapter 3

God Confidence

Can miracles occur? Are they happening in front of us daily? Have we experienced miracles but never knew it? Can he know our thoughts and feelings and be so in tune with us that our every function in life is tied to him?

Could we have established contact with a being so vast and powerful yet willing to listen to our requests that we're in awe of him? If God were an alien, would we be more likely to listen to him and believe he existed? Would it frighten us if God granted our requests? What if we asked for something so big and great that it had no explanation except a miraculous one?

Can you imagine God intervening in your life in response to your request? Almost sounds like a movie in which special effects make it look as if magic just occurred. Except with God, there are no special effects or blue screens or computers involved.

Do we need genies and Santa Claus? What about if we close our eyes and imagine we have powers we can summon at the blink of an eye? Would that be a miracle? Can we summon spirits from the deep? Maybe in fiction, but not in the real world. Fairy tales have led us down the wrong path to a magical world that's fun to follow but still the stuff of fairy tales.

With the ever-present God, there is no need for magic.

What would you pray to God for if you thought he might answer your prayer? What miracle would you ask God to perform? What help would you ask him for as you face a world full of unknowns? What would you consider a gift from God? You'd find the list to be very long if you wrote down the possibilities.

Let's suppose you asked God for more confidence. Would receiving more confidence be a miracle? It might not be your first request, but it should be among them. Confidence lies deep within ourselves, and God can activate it. Can we believe in ourselves if we don't believe in God? It seems as if believing God could give you confidence is not out of the question. A God who knows you and your best and worst attributes and is still willing to answer your prayer for more confidence seems possible. If you believe in only yourself, you may have placed a limitation on your confidence. An unlimited God could remove those limitations and boost your confidence. If you're being interviewed for a job, taking the ice as a figure skater, or walking on stage to sing in an opera, your confidence has to go through the roof. And it will if it's God given.

If we don't believe in ourselves, nobody else will. If we don't have belief, we cannot function very well doing the ordinary things in life. We must believe in our driving skills to maneuver in traffic, but can we have too much confidence when we drive? Confidence can control our thinking and maybe save our lives at some point. We must be physically and mentally skillful beings when we drive.

This same confidence is required when we ask God for miracles because that's a form of faith that goes beyond believing to a level that makes us feel God is with us. Such confidence creates an energy beyond our earthly doubts and fears. When we are in danger, we can call upon God with a feeling that he is there and can and will help us. The tightness in our chests we feel when we drive is because of our fear of getting in an accident. God needs to be with us when we apply the brakes or steer our way around another car.

We are not the creator; we are the created. We may soon be able to make replicas of ourselves and transfer our old selves into new selves. But until that day comes, we're stuck in our bodies. We will still face the day when we must exist in a spirit form rather than a bodily form and face eternity. "And God shall wipe away all tears from their eyes; and there shall be no more death, neither sorrow, nor crying, neither shall there be any more pain; for the former things are passed away" (Revelation 21:4 KJV).

With the confidence God can give us, we can move forward knowing we're capable of overcoming anything because we'll believe he will be with us. We can touch a leaf as it blows gently by us because we have the God confidence that keeps us in tune with all that exists. When we travel into space, we'll be able to respond properly to everything we face.

Don't look in the mirror expecting to see a confident person. You may not like what you see and get discouraged. Don't constantly monitor your confidence or abilities. Be confident with God's help. Your personal confidence is not the same as God confidence. God wants you to believe in yourself as well as in him; he will sustain your confidence. You can't sing better, or dance better, or play a sport better by yourself. You need God's help.

Ask God to place a blanket of confidence over you through sincere prayer. Let every day make you better than yesterday, and tomorrow, you'll be even better because God's confidence in you will grow as you grow. Strive to grow in knowledge and abilities. Strive to find skills that you can do better than others. Look for what you can do best.

Read the Bible and learn of those who had confidence. Though they are gone, they are still your teachers. They are examples of how God helps people, and he can help you as well. You were made by him, and you belong to him. You are made of the earth he created, and you live because of him.

When at last someone sets foot on a distant planet, God confidence will go along. Let his confidence govern your interplanetary dwelling place. Carry it strongly in your mind and body, and do not deny it or run from it. Accept it and embrace it.

No matter the task or the challenge, reach inside for the confidence God put there. When you fall, rise. Fight to your last breath; God will be there with you. Be encouraged every day by the confidence you have, and welcome the God-given confidence that lets you do the impossible. Keep getting up after you've been knocked down. Call on God to renew your strength. That will make you a believer in the confidence only God can give.

Instill God confidence in others. Your family needs confidence as do children who have no one to tell them about God confidence. Pass out God confidence as though it's free money. Be patient with others who don't have your determination to achieve. Teach determination that leads others to places they never imagined they could get to. Teach and tell others of God confidence, then sit back and let God teach them. Watch others succeed as they learn what you have learned. God's confidence is abundant, so use it as you would a new power you received. It's a miracle in you that needs to be awakened in a technological world. It's like a super-human power carrying you to the stars and beyond. Don't look back, and never doubt you can achieve.

Ask God questions about your confidence. He will answer you in ways you never imagined. He may answer you in the concert hall or on the playing field, but he will not only answer, he will also show you your weaknesses and lack of faith in yourself and him. God's answers will give you even more confidence as you grow in God confidence and seek greater successes.

We are mortal beings, but mortal attuned to immortal makes us powerful and successful in the end.

Chapter 4

Awakening Others

The disciples questioned Jesus constantly because they didn't understand his powers. They wanted to do as he did, and they eventually became more like him. Because they questioned God in a constructive way—asking the right questions—they received power to preach and teach and heal through God and his confidence. They became students of God and attained the highest level possible of God confidence, which becomes faith in God. God was tutoring them until they knew enough to be on their own.

He will tutor you as well; he will be there with you when others say something can't be done. But you will do it because you awakened a miracle and you awakened to God.

Failures become your teachers. When you assume you know everything, you may be brought to your knees. Failures teach us everything from learning to walk and talk to how to walk with a cane in old age. Never let a failure change your life. Don't bend or break because you failed; consider it a great lesson that no money or training could buy. Failure teaches as does success. Do it better next time. You failed because you knew what failure was, and by knowing the face of failure, you'll never want to see it again. Let the next time and the next time teach you not to fail.

You will find God to be very patient; his teaching will never end. He wants you to succeed to show you he cares for you. If you quit, you may blame God. No need to blame God if you quit. You become the quitter, not God. Ask him to show you again and again. The answer is there. "And I say unto you, Ask, and it shall be given you, seek, and ye shall find; knock, and it shall be opened unto you" (Luke 11:9 KJV).

God is pleased when you succeed. Reaching and touching success is magic beyond our definition of magic. It's also humbling. When you reach the pinnacle, you'll want more because that's the way God works. You'll seek yet higher levels of success; that will become a way of life. You'll desire to find more of what God gives; you'll always be reaching out for that next invention, device, or method of performing surgery better or discovering what you can do better than anyone else.

With God's help, we can take on challenges and make the world better. May we never stop fine tuning ourselves and trying new things. God's help can carry us through life. We found him, and he found us. Awaken the miracle of confidence in others as you tell them about God. Some won't listen, but others will.

Championship teams' coaches teach their players how to play the game individually and as members of a team. The players' levels of confidence rise as their belief in themselves and as members of a team rises. Add God confidence to that, and the players become far better. Those who are successful in winning become successful in believing in themselves in the present and the future.

Don't expect others to show you gratitude just because you taught them about God confidence. People may be on the brink of bankruptcy or on the edge of giving up totally and you come along and teach them about God, and one day, you meet them as successful people and they barely recognize you.

Some people may be so heavily into drugs that it may seem helping them would be a waste of time. Persevere. Don't give up on the human spirit, for those you help will become new one day. With the power of God confidence, people can overcome great obstacles.

Just be the messenger; let them receive your message. Leave it up to them and God how it will take place. Don't be surprised at how many people will come back to you for help. It takes only a little bit of your energy to help others, but it may take a lot of energy on their part to get beyond their problems. Compliment people you help; that can prompt the greatest progress of all in them.

Lean into people mentally if you're trying to help them. Listen attentively to others. Listen to their doubts, problems, and concerns. Discover why they don't believe in themselves. Attack their unbelief at the root. Take away their reasons for not believing they can attain God confidence. Give them something that gives them a reason to succeed. Find out what excites them and makes them dream big. Build on their hopes and dreams until they become reality. Find out whom they respect, whom they want to be like, and build their confidence on that. Let them know that God confidence is a whole new level of confidence.

If those you lean into in this way aren't interested, seek out people who want, need, and appreciate what you can do for them. Children especially want help because they feel helpless. Give them a memento to remind them—a picture, or a bracelet, or a T-shirt with a phrase on it such as "Someday" or "Believe." Let them know what they're trying to do is real and you appreciate their efforts. "If it's to be, it's up to me" is a good one.

Chapter 5

Sound the Trumpet

You can use the Internet to find those who need the help you can offer. Use the Internet as much as you can because it may be their language; it may be where they look for something new and fresh to help them. Let them find you, a source of hope and inspiration. Let them find whatever makes their lives better. Just point them in the right direction. Let them find confidence and success. It's their choice to find God. The Internet may help them, but teach them to pray and you will have taught them the greatest skill anyone can teach.

Don't just meet them. Get to know them. Encourage them to let you know their needs and problems. What do they love? Whom do they love? Who is important in their lives? Look for the person among the rubble. Look for the person behind the person, the one who needs your help. Reach out and let God show you that person. They may be fragile, so be kind, soft, and gentle with them. Talk them through their tears and fears; don't give up on them.

Prisons are filled with people who didn't believe anyone cared. Dig down into such people; they need your understanding. Consider it a mining expedition; you're digging for people who badly need your help. How do you get them out of the mine and into the sunlight where God can give them his confidence and show them how to change their lives? God's light turns on the light in their heads; that makes them want what you have.

The people you help may be runaways, or divorcees, or the perpetrators of acts they can't forgive themselves for. You need to keep an open mind about all people; your life can be in danger from some people, but don't show fear. Work with people who can become overcomers and leave the lost by the wayside. Leaving someone behind is tough to do, but realize that God hasn't finished with them yet. Let others reach out where you've left off. You can't help everyone, but your help may be so strong that a teaspoon of it could be a shovelful to some people.

Think of yourself as an awakener of miracles as you reach out to others to awaken what's deep inside them. You'll be rewarded by seeing them succeed and becoming a success yourself. You can be the alarm clock that wakes certain people up to their inherent gifts from God. Awaken others to the greatest gift they may ever receive, and watch as God does his work with them. Direct people's lives to what you think they can do best, but don't overlook something that pops up later; people have hidden talents, so be open minded about those you help. The most you may ever get from anyone is a hug or a big thank you, but be happy for that because it may be a struggle to get that.

Sometimes, people idolize someone they once knew or wanted to know. Listen to their whole story from beginning to end. Bring back to life the person they idolize by getting them to live through what made that other person great. Be unique in your God confidence and show them your versatility to accept their heroes or idols. Maybe get them concert tickets or tickets to a baseball or football game. Show you care by using whatever you can to convince them they will become people with God confidence. Let them come alive.

Chapter 6

Beyond the Mirror

Be strong for yourself and others. Ask God to brace you with steel pillars that will withstand any storm. You may be the kind of person who becomes so involved in other people's problems that they take you down to their level, but your God confidence can counter that. You may feel something for others because you've been through what they're going through—drugs or some other weakness—but you can reach inside and find the strength to get them through it as well.

Look to the scriptures for help often; they are your teachers too. Many scriptures are right on when it comes to our problems. Use the Bible as handbook or guidebook or map or whatever it needs to be for your life and the lives of those you're trying to help.

We have unbelievable inner strength. God confidence with God strength is a powerful combination; believe in it and trust it even in your or anyone else's darkest hours. The confidence within must be awakened often and renewed as God gives you and others strength. Pray to God for his confidence and strength. Walk into a room and look around. Everyone may be staring at you wondering how you can have so much confidence. Hold seminars or give talks at churches, schools, or wherever people listen. Walk and move in his gift of confidence and never lose it. Do what you do best—music, sports, work, or play—with his confidence and guidance.

We're talking about areas below the radar screen we see ourselves in. We look in the mirror and are surprised at what we see. We look for a nice person, but our eyes are drawn to hairs out of place or blemishes and are upset with the flaws we see.

Suppose we could see beyond the mirror to our subconscious selves. Suppose we were horrified to see what lies deep in us. Could we accept that person? Yet that is part of who we are. We get x-rayed and undergo all sorts of tests. We go on diets and start exercising to fix what ails us. Under the surface of who and what we are lies an untested area we can't see. Psychiatrists can analyze us and place labels on us, but our real selves are often hidden from analysis. We may find more than one person in us, in some instances several types of people who are quite different from one another. This seems fixable, but the human mind may function one way today and another way tomorrow.

Chapter 7

A Greater Person

We can be influenced by other people and what they say. We're bombarded with information, but only bits and pieces of it may make sense to us. We become members of churches or other social groups often with the best of intentions. Then one day, something triggers our subconscious to do something completely out of character and we suddenly believe we're that person rather than the one we remember. Are we who we believe we are? Is the mirror now suddenly in focus that shows us the real person we were born to be? We may have awakened our confidence; we may have discovered in our subconscious someone greater than the one we knew.

God has a way of showing us facets of ourselves we never knew existed. God can awaken our subconscious to new and stronger depths many times in our lives. In this realm of the mind, the mystical, inner self comes alive with confidence we never knew existed. That might be nice, but some people believe themselves to be Napoleon or someone of great prominence; that's the reason some end up in institutions.

Might we look to other possible sources of who we are? Are we looking for the mirror that tells us who or what is deep inside? Some people may not wish to enter that part of themselves afraid of what or whom they might see. It's not a trip to another planet or back in time but a journey within that may reveal our hidden talents and powers.

It's like going into the mine of the mind to just look around. No need to rearrange anything because this is just a discovery mission. Should you find a resource, you can go back later for its strength and value. You may be disappointed, or you may be very happy to find the good and the bad, but just by looking in the mirror of yourself, you may feel better about yourself.

What can you look for? Your emotions for one thing. Which emotion is dominant in your life? Do you see your emotions as a big part of yourself, or are you an unemotional person and therefore very calm? Sort of like a moon rover or robotic traveler looking at the surface of a planet. What else do you see besides emotion? Do you see beliefs?

So many things are in our beliefs and what we base our decisions upon. Are we informed about those beliefs? At what point are our beliefs satisfied?

Chapter 8

Talent

In the microcosmic center of the universe within us, we seek to find what God has secretly put there. We don't know what's there just as we don't know the secrets of the planets, moons, and stars. We know a very little about ourselves, but how much of ourselves is so deep in our minds that we don't know about it?

In our brains are things we never knew existed. The Bible says that if we seek, we will find. Seek the treasure in the mind; that's where the real gold and silver lie.

As science explores the planets, moons, and stars, we must seek within ourselves diligently to discover what we're capable of and what we want to be capable of. The mind has a decision maker in it by which we decide what to do and when to do it. We decide how to think, what to accept and reject, and what to believe. We decide if God is real or a fantasy.

If you decide to mine within yourself, quite likely you'll want the creator of your mind to help you understand what is there. Your ancestors have contributed to your genetic structure, but they and their capabilities are now unknown. Seek out your capabilities within. Test yourself in different fields of endeavor. Are you good at music, or politics, or public speaking? Are you good at helping others as a doctor or a nurse would? Are you good at being a missionary or a college professor? Are you a welder or mechanic? We cannot be sure what we are good at, but chances are we're good or better at some things than others. Test yourself to see what capabilities and tendencies you have. You'll be surprised to meet who you are and happy you can be doing what you like with confidence. Let God awaken the miracle in you.

Are you just a decision maker, or do you look deep within and discover different aspects of yourself? Ask God to unlock the hidden secrets in your mind. Ask God to give you the code to yourself. You may find you travel into one part of your mind only to find you want to enter an even deeper part of yourself.

How deep in the mind can we go? Is the brain simply a right-left mechanism connected by a corpus callosum that automatically exchanges information between the two hemispheres? Why would we accept that? When we turn on our computers or cell phones, are we responding robotically? Are we automatically stuck at the same level and engaging in revolving-door thinking? Are we hypnotically going around and around in our minds when we're on the Internet? Can we break out of that hypnotic state and set ourselves free? Will we break free from politically correct group thinking? Would we be allowed by that group to even imagine God exists?

With so much information, who needs God? It doesn't matter if Internet information is correct. What's the next step of mind control if we can call the Internet that? Could the Internet replace itself with a freethinking mechanism that helps us dig deep within ourselves? What device could help us plumb the depths of our minds and become the next Einstein, or maestro, or leader of our country? How can we improve on devices so they help us free ourselves rather than train us to believe what we read on the Internet?

What if all the books in a giant library were slanted in the way that library wants us to think? Some of the books could be accurate, but others could be steering mechanisms to make us believe something that's just not true. Would there be any books in that library other than the Bible that say God exists?

The fact that God exists doesn't have to be in a book. We can see his creation all around us in trees, flowers, birds, and the rest of nature. Did we create the sky, or the earth, or ourselves? Who then did? That's an Internet question, a classroom question, but it doesn't have a satisfactory answer other than the simplest answer— God made us. Whether he used a big bang or simply spoke it into existence doesn't matter.

Can the depths of our mind control whether we lose weight? The secret of losing weight, or gaining strength, or becoming an Olympic runner lies in the depths of the subconscious. If we allow ourselves to do things automatically, we somehow know things. How can a person walk a tightrope without a net? How can someone survive an unsurvivable accident? Can it be that God is involved in the things that show us what we can do if we believe and try? The subconscious mind may be where many miracles happen; we never think about the fact that we can walk upright, or sing, or talk, or do complex math problems. The subconscious may hold secrets we'll never discover unless we travel there.

Chapter 9

Will We Benefit?

We must be ready when the world changes into something we never expected it to become. Will we travel by high-speed trains, buses, or autos? Will we even need transportation as it now exists? Will we simply travel through visual devices that make it seem we have actually traveled but through technology we never leave our homes? Will we travel in vehicles that levitate quietly through distances around the world? Will our best friends live in other countries? Will we have devices that break all languages into thought waves that allow us to communicate simply with gestures? These are interesting concepts we must prepare ourselves for so we can provide for ourselves and families and get from point to point.

Herein lie the secret, subconscious reactions to a new world beyond anything we imagined but we adjust to using our minds. We may even be able to communicate through telepathy. Let us prepare our minds for the future. Let the Internet help us as God helps us. Let technology help us with the devices we will need, and let it all demonstrate God's glory.

To live in such a technologically advanced world requires high IQs of course, but it also requires us to be able to persuade others to agree with us and function from within ourselves. It may be that in our subconscious mind lie the abilities to do so automatically.

Chapter 10

Auto-Respond

An auto-response system may be the next step toward our future. We admire people who excel at sports; they don't stop to gather data about a catch they're trying to make; they don't take surveys about how to make a catch—they simply go on autopilot and catch it. Their hours and hours of practice have developed that capability in them. They react. They make the catch.

Our confidence and auto-response systems control our lives now, but will that be sufficient for us in the future? Will we be able to react quickly enough or intelligently enough? Can God intervene in our internal mechanisms and make us quicker, better, or more successful? Will he require us to speed up our responses, or will he give us a chance to slow everything down to our age and ability level?

The future will be different from today. Responses to simply driving an automobile may be handled by higher-intelligence systems that can perform beyond our skill levels. Think of fighter pilots who can black out when modern jets exceed their abilities to withstand tremendous G forces; a robot wouldn't worry about that.

Imagine your great-grandparents struggling to do something that has become so easy today due to technological advances. We have upgraded our skills through technology, but will we need one of God's miracles to go beyond our physical restraints? Do we need to concentrate on awakening inner miracles? What are the stress levels going to be in such a world? If we cannot operate devices, can we adjust with medications that keep us calm, or should we seek answers within? Is it possible that in the depths of the subconscious medications are no longer needed?

That's what the future holds for us. We can overcome whatever controls us whether it be drugs, alcohol, medications, or just our disbelief in our abilities to get there from here. Are we supposed to be our own worst enemy? Better to be confident and attuned to what God shows us we can be and then strive to be healthier and happier than ever before.

Chapter 11

A Technological World and God

Deep within ourselves is an information center so vast that computers cannot control it or predict it. Advertisers seek to reach this center and convince us to buy their products. But in the depths of the mind, we lie in another world. Social skills live in the depths of the mind; the ability to hide who we are may lie hidden for years before suddenly appearing in a news headline somewhere, and people are shocked that humans are capable of such things. It's better for newspapers to report when we are successful and report it correctly.

Are the automatic responses within us tied somehow to God? Were these responses put in us to allow us to function properly now and in the future? Could we function without automatic responses? With the help of God, can these automatic responses be multiplied or amplified sufficiently to allow us to react quicker or more intelligently than we ever imagined we could? What hinders our automatic responses and allows us to engage in radically different social behavior and harm ourselves or others? Can it be that without God, we disconnect and have psychotic episodes?

In a world in which people could make an atomic bomb in a garage and destroy cities because God told them to, what morality exists that would prevent such a thing from happening? Are not lone-wolf bombings now more likely to happen than world wars?

People are often underestimated; what lies in the subconscious must somehow be able to function within the limits of world order and the desire for peace; it can't be allowed to prompt an individual to shut the entire system down due to an auto-response.

We assume we'll always be safe no matter what because of technology, but technology itself may cause our destruction. We need a God who controls what happens every day. We need sanity and confidence to live our lives freely and enjoyably. We need to auto-respond in ways that don't destroy us. Through God, we can find that these forces work together and promote successful and happy lives. Seek the miracle of awakening the self within that is powerful enough to want to live in peace and protect others along the way.

We also need confidence in our inner selves to connect with others' confidence and inner selves. We have to function together on certain things for everyone's safety despite our disagreements. Safety first. That applies today and will do so long into the future. We can teach ourselves and others to live side by side yet apart and create an even better world.

Chapter 12

What Is Our Limitation?

With God's help, we can look to a greater power who understands our needs and helps all who are starving at God's table and want just a few crumbs from it. We don't need a supercomputer; we need the super God who created us and knows the number of hairs on our heads and everything else about us.

At that point in our existence as humans, we can advance and create. The most awesome part of God to some people is the way he creates everything from sunrises to distant nebulae. Researching ancient scrolls for the secrets of the past is fine if they are analyzed properly. What we need is a roadmap for our future so vast we cannot compute it. God needs to give us the roadmap now; we need to progress. That roadmap belongs to God, who in his infinite wisdom can guide us every day and lead us to secrets of the universe and stars and beyond.

We need a roadmap connected to our inner selves that goes beyond the level of computers and science into the world of miracles. He can guide us to the simplest of functions or to answers why children can die and why the elderly succumb to diseases of the mind and body. We need a God who can guide us into a world in which we can live longer and healthier lives. We need a miracle that will carry us far into the future.

We all have within us inner persons capable of controlling us and making us powerful. Maybe the inner person is who we must be to live in a world of robotics and technology. A robot can do many things, but can it reason? Can a robot make decisions on the spot that save a baby from a burning building? Instant reactions must be programmed into robots or computers. We must become better than the robots or the computers we design; with God's miracle help, we can control our future.

What hidden powers do we have? Houdini believed in the subconscious. He believed in a mystical self and a world he could manage. He put on straightjackets, had himself locked in trunks, and allowed himself to be thrown into rivers. One time, he didn't come up out of the trunk or river; the mystery lives on whether he escaped.

Can we lift a car off a child as has been said a mother once did? What superhuman qualities do we have? When we connect those superhuman qualities with those God has shown us in the Bible, can we slay a Goliath? Can we perform miracles? Is there a place within where we connect with God but deny its existence for fear of the social consequences? Might we be subject to ridicule if we did something miraculous? People have been burned at the stake for saying God had spoken to them, and others were locked away as lunatics or devils for such things. What was destroyed in the Dark Ages as books were burned? What if we had that knowledge and found it helpful? Suppose we could travel back in time. Would we be able to handle not changing the things that shaped history?

Chapter 13

Can We Control Our Future?

Time travel is just an example of how we might react to the future. What if we could change the future by creating something so dramatic that it might make cell phones things of the past? What capabilities do we have locked in ourselves? Have we sold ourselves short in what could be or what could have been had we shared an idea or invention with the rest of the world?

What lies just below the tip of the iceberg of our minds? Can we control our genetics by thought, or can we control our genomes by researching the body and finding a link that destroys some disease scientifically? Do we all have hidden computers in us that are constantly analyzing what we think are simple answers to problems only to find out they are extremely difficult to program into a robotic creation or to duplicate technologically?

What we call instincts may be something we know very little about. Why do we call them instincts? Are we just guessing or imagining things? Do our instincts often save our lives? If they do, where in the brain do we find instincts? Are instincts more of an imaginary way we invent what we're going to do because we're bored?

Deep in our minds, we fear heights, germs, crowds, noises we don't recognize, and many other things. Our fears may be imaginary, but they're real as far as we're concerned. What if we look to God and find our fears have gone away? What if we even attack our fears and overcome them with the help of God?

If we incorporate God into our minds, what are we truly capable of doing? Did people in the Bible carry God in their minds as real as they did their fears? There were certainly things to fear in biblical times, but God has given us many things to defend ourselves since the days of swords. The future could be as different as the past is. What dangers do we face and not even know? What weapons of tomorrow could have saved us today? "Take therefore no thought for the morrow; for the morrow shall take thought for the things of itself. Sufficient unto the day is the evil thereof" (Matthew 6:34 KJV).

Optimism and hope are other factors we might consider besides confidence and our inner selves. We all hope everyday goes well, that all our ducks line up. They do line up, but not always in the way we expect. We have a concept of how our day should go only to find out that it turned out quite different.

The unpredictable things that clutter up our day often end up taking most of the day to take care of, and then we look up and ask, "Where did the time go?" Some random act or acts occur and we're suddenly off track and sailing right along. And then it suddenly seems maybe that was meant to be and we're glad it happened.

What if God is the one in control and you only think you can control your day? What if your day was planned long ago and you couldn't change it no matter what? Maybe it's a God thing you wanted to control your day, but whatever happened just happened and the day is gone. And all your previous days too. You can't change the inevitable.

Should we blame God for our day as though he had interrupted it? Did he place us somewhere on a path we didn't want to be on? What purpose would God have for doing that? Unless he is steering us toward something good. Surely, a loving God will not steer us toward the rocks. Should we look to God in prayer and ask for his help often throughout the day to keep us on track of where we should be? And just where should we be? What purpose do our lives have? Can God make us follow his path? Why would God want that? Is his path better? More tolerable than ours?

Maybe we don't know where we're going, but God does. Maybe that train could have hit our car except something delayed us. Maybe that boy wouldn't have run in front of your car if his mother had called him. Maybe that explosion in a restaurant you left ten minutes ago could have gone off ten minutes sooner. Maybe he's trying to save your life. How many times has he saved your life and you never knew it? Seconds end up saving lives every day.

A stick floating in a river can be carried a long way, even out to sea. We're carried by the forces that surround us. Why would we think we could control the river of time and space? Why and how can we defy the laws of physics that control the ebb and flow of our lives? What forces can we use to help steer us through life?

Randomness simply throws a direction at us, and we follow it until it lets us off and another random force sends us somewhere else. Suppose God can control random forces. Suppose God can control outcomes in our lives. Can prayer have a physical effect on us and steer us in a direction that's best for us? Can the depths of our minds mysteriously move us in such a way that God's miracles awaken us to moments that allow us to live another day?

Chapter 14

How Do We Move a Mountain?

All we can do is pray and hope. Hope comes with optimism and not just through positive thinking, which is close, but sheer optimism along with hope becomes faith. The Bible says faith can move a mountain; it must be a powerful force. Believe that faith can be a force that moves mountains and faith will become a force we can use every day.

Faith is optimistic, and hope looks to the possibility that something great could happen. Faith then becomes a substance and a force that can move things. Nothing we know can move a mountain except heavy equipment and then only in bits and pieces. Faith can be a force we build upon and learn how to use. We may have to try a million times to conquer faith, but once we realize it's based on hope and optimism, we have begun that powerful journey. Is there a force in the universe greater than faith?

What's so amazing is that we can create faith within ourselves. How powerful are we? What disasters have we prevented just by faith? What miracle can we awaken in our world today? What can we conquer in the future?

Chapter 15

Are You Cheating Yourself?

Are you cheating yourself out of miracles? Are you talking yourself out of possibly allowing God to create a miracle in your life? Is someone else convincing you to stick with science only? Why not give God a chance to show you just how miraculous he can be in your everyday life?

Find something to ask God to do that isn't something you can control. You may have a sick relative not responding to medication, or you may have an incurable disease. Make it be a miracle. You will know it was he who did it. When you know the miracle has taken place, look to God with thanksgiving. Only God can do miracles, but he may use someone or something to do it. Quite possibly, nobody else but yourself will be involved. Listen to God as he answers your prayer. God won't ask you to do something dangerous, so know the difference between a miracle and a delusional suggestion. You will feel something that tells you it was of God.

Ever seen what terrible days negative people can have? The last thing they believe seems to be that a miracle could ever take place. They believe in the bad things that happen so much that they even tell everyone, "Bad things happen, so watch out!" It seems that's their life mission. Bad things that happen to them are never their fault. Don't be around such people because they may bring destruction down on you. Be careful whom your friends are, and be optimistic with anyone who is all doom and gloom. Optimism will always win over negativism.

Circumstances develop into one calamity after another sometimes, so look for the negative person, the unbeliever, and then look to God for a miracle. Look for the person who is pulling negative energy into the room. God's miracles don't usually happen to naysayers; there must be a belief or optimism. There must be hope no matter the situation.

You can end up lost in the woods even when you were just out for a stroll. God doesn't want us to be lost; we choose to be lost. Maintaining our optimism is a big help no matter where we are and no matter what we face. We hear bad news—maybe about a child lost in a mall—and we panic. We hope for the best, but hope alone won't find the child. But if you're optimistic, your senses will work better.

Chapter 16

Can You Feel His Hand?

As we go into the future, we think of progress and hope for devices that will help us become better able to handle our daily lives. Whatever the future holds, we should maintain our optimism. By faith, we can ask God for the future to unfold before us in such a marvelous way that even scientists will be amazed. Whether we're exploring a distant planet or moon, we need to remain optimistic. We may be on a basketball team that hasn't won a game all season, but we should be optimistic. We may find that when we shoot a basketball with optimism, it goes in the basket more often than if we are pessimistic about that possibility. Optimism is contagious; it's not just hoping or positive thinking but believing we can accomplish something.

If we're less-than-optimistic astronauts, we might not get off the launch pad; if we're optimistic and look to God, we might just succeed. God's presence tells us we're not alone.. He is nearby, and we sense it, but how can we know? Something inside tells us he is near.

> I can feel his hand upon my hand
> I can tell that he is near

I cannot see him
I feel him by my side
I can only hope that through my life here he does abide

—Kenneth Foley

Chapter 17

God Awakens in Us

With God in charge of our optimism, we can become more confident. We need not doubt outcomes; we simply stay in his will and follow what we feel he wants us to do. Always maintaining a smiling, optimistic approach to whatever we do asking God to be involved in. Always asking God for that miracle and see if it awakens in us.

Just to awaken each day is a miracle, but to awaken with God is a miracle beyond description. The first thing we should do is reach out to God in thanks and let hope and optimism enter us as we praise God. The world can measure all it wants, but the results are what counts.

Can you reach your goals by yourself? Can you go way past that goal to higher goals than you ever believed with God? Did anyone believe a little boy with only a sling and some rocks could slay a giant?

Don't doubt your God but synchronize with him through prayer and defy the laws of physics and opinions of others. Who cares what others believe? It's your belief that counts. If certain others people could prevent a miracle, oddly enough, they would. Forgive their unbelief.

What hope can anyone in solitary confinement have? In a dark place with just a metal cot and four walls. Hope and optimism can fade very fast if that person doesn't call on God for help. He can hope that just by scratching at his walls bit by bit every day will one day years and years later allow him to escape and see the light of day.

But God can penetrate any wall instantly. And your optimism can do the same. With faith, you can reach places you never imagined. Optimism can save anyone; the human spirit functions much better with optimism, which evokes peace that passes all understanding and will prevail even against the gates of hell.

Our spirits cannot be broken if we don't allow that to happen. Even in the face of physical torture, we must look to God for inner strength. That is where the miracle in us awakens, but we need not wait that long for the miracle of God in us to awaken. We need to find God long before we suffer pain and imprisonment of any kind. He wants his miracles to awaken our sense of connection between our souls and him.

Hope beyond reason and understanding comes as a result of perfect optimism. God doesn't care about our understanding; he just does what we ask him to do. Faith is where we meet God. On the empty desert of the mind we wander and one day find God. He is not a mirage. He opens his arms to us and welcomes us home. God doesn't survey the world for others' approval to welcome us; he just does. He does what's necessary, and he knows our needs and wonders what took us so long to come to him for help.

Faith is reaching God through a doorway to our new home with God. Faith is a doorway that opens if we but turn the handle of our minds and open that door by believing.

Chapter 18

Do We Sabotage Our Beliefs?

We are so busy that we cannot ask God for a simple thing like being with us this day in all we do. We cannot ask him to watch over us or be with us. We are scientific and therefore can do without God as long as we have our cell phones, automobiles, and computers.

Then one day, we realize that was not all we needed. We listened to ourselves as we lied to ourselves and went on with life and found out what life without God was like. Eternity is like that; we could be alone without God.

The Bible spells it out for us. We believe that if we think positive thoughts, we won't need God, but we're lying to ourselves. We deny God entry into our lives and the chance to perform miracles that would change everything for the better. We do not need to know the law of gravity to understand that gravity works. And so does God. What can God do? He spoke the world into existence. He can speak your miracle into existence if you but believe.

We can sabotage our lives by wrong thinking and wrong beliefs that lead to wrong decisions and wrong actions. That dangerous way to live will catch up to us one day, and then we seek God, and then we find he was there all the time. The strange thing is that he will still listen to us just as he listened to the thief on the cross. But there is no need for us to wait until our lives are nearly over when we can live much happier and more wonderful lives with God's help.

Do we choose our destinies? Is it our decision to travel the low road or the difficult road, or is someone controlling us? The low road is lonely, and we look to others for approval. We never reach the point where everyone likes what we do, but we cannot please everyone.

When you walk with God, you walk the high road and you don't have to please everyone because he will show you the way. You must be committed to walk the high road because it is difficult and trying at times even with God, but without him, life can be intolerable. Your commitment to God determines your future. When you set foot on another planet, it will be your commitment to God, who sustains you if he is with you by your choice. When you travel at speeds beyond what you now perceive as fast, you need God with you. Across the universe or across town, you need him with you.

If you will commit to living for him, he will always be with you. God knows your heart and intentions, and he will help you every day. You may need split-second timing to turn or stop, but God can grant you that. He can also give you better health and more happiness and help you accept the things that cause distress. An uncertain future can be mind boggling, but if you grow into an unlimited future, with God's help, you can do anything.

Chapter 19

Two Kinds of People

Let the enemy of our spirits cover his ears because of our prayers. Let our prayers come forth like a mighty waterfall before God's throne, and may he hear our prayers. May we move into the future with the greatest of all powers within us.

There are two kinds of people—those with a fire within and those who try to extinguish others' fires. The fire within came down on the day of Pentecost. Like a great and mighty force of wind, it came into the upper room. The disciples saw tongues of fire come down and rest on each of them, and they began to speak in other tongues. Which of course was a mighty miracle. Jesus had said that would happen after he had arisen. That miracle negated the curse of the Tower of Babel temporarily for them.

We don't have to wait in any upper room for those tongues of fire; they come down constantly to ignite our inner being. When we awaken to God and receive his fire, we are transformed; the scales fall from our eyes and we awake to a miracle.

We do not need to run around speaking to others in other languages, but anything's possible with God. We all have inner flames that go with us when we die. Our souls, however, are eternal. We live our lives and enjoy the wonderful things God has given us. Some people's flames are barely flickering as they hang onto life day by day. Other people's flames glow so brightly that when they walk into the room, you feel its joyful radiance and share in it.

But others will try to douse that flame with their negativity. They give into the urge to give such people sad news. It seems impossible that there are people who wish the worst would happen, but it seems true. Avoid them for they can only bring you down; they cannot rise above their way of thinking and feeling. If you could change them, that would be a miracle in itself. They seek the negative, minute particles of life that most people never think about and avoid naturally. These kind hang onto little, ugly tidbits and sayings so tightly it's like the "from my cold, dead hands" slogan of those who will never give up their guns. What is easier to understand than pure hate coming from someone teaching others to hate others? Or to feel they've accomplished something with their anger, rage, and jealousy because they hate the innocence of those who believe God can and will listen to prayer?

God's flame is not so different from the flame of life though it adds to the flame like an afterburner. Something happens to those people when that flame begins to burn in them. It's a happy flame that does what nobody ever expected it to do. God's flame inspires us from within. We see people in time of war who rise to the occasion and become heroes. We see firemen run into burning buildings to save people. We saw them on TV as they ran into the World Trade Center and gave their lives.

In the ordinary course of living, we need that flame to rescue one another from tragedies and sadness. We need to be something to someone else and save them. When others lose hope, they need people who have the flame within. We need to ask God to rescue those in need. People who are ready to walk out the door and never come back need the help of someone who has God's flame within. Almost every day, some need us to tell them they are worthwhile and shouldn't give up. When we even smell the smoke of someone afraid of life, we should let God's hand touch him or her through us.

When you speak to them, let God speak the precious words only he through you can to change a negative or bad situation into something good for that person.

Chapter 20

A Fire That Inspires

The fire God gives us is often one spoken to motivate others at graduation speeches or in election campaigns. The fire God gives can come from a child who says, "Please, mister, help me!" And they have nobody else to turn to. Don't pass up the greatest of life's opportunities. We were put here to help one another through our crises.

God's fire may come from a pulpit where a pastor, priest, or rabbi says something that cuts to the bone of the congregation, which realizes those words were meant for them. Maybe God's fire comes at halftime in a championship game and the players go on to win despite the odds.

We can attain the fire of God daily in our lives and love it. Others can't wait to be uninspired by the news and negative words they live by. We are not the little train that said "I think I can, I think I can." It's not a matter of us determining the fire and how hot it will be and how much it will inspire us, but we should let it come to us in many ways. We can let God's fire ignite something in us even if it's just to lose weight or walk across the room.

Music is one way we can be inspired. What music inspires you? What singers inspire you? What songs inspire you? How often we feel the words of "Amazing Grace" fan that fire in us. Music is one way to be inspired. The rest of life is at times just another log on the fireplace of life that keeps our flames burning. God's fire is a living thing, and we feel it deep inside. It feels wonderful, and we hunger for it. We can get by on food and water, but once we've tasted God's fire, we can't live without it. We want more and more of it. Music can bring that fire to us, and sometimes, that's the only way we can feel that God fire. Music is a miracle gift of God.

We can also be inspired by others' words. People can inspire people. Just as we can be uninspired by others' anger and hate, we can inspire and light the fire that starts as a spark or thought or feeling and grows into a flame that burns bright in our soul. What magic does this? Only God's magic because it is the magic of the soul. God's magic is in us and comes alive under the words or music of others. We should sit at the feet of those who inspire us. Why don't we seek those people out? Why won't they share their inspirational thoughts, writings, and songs more often? Were they not inspired as they worked to inspire others? Too often, we lose inspiring singers and musicians. What a tragedy. Look to God. He won't let you down. We let him down too often, but he still loves us.

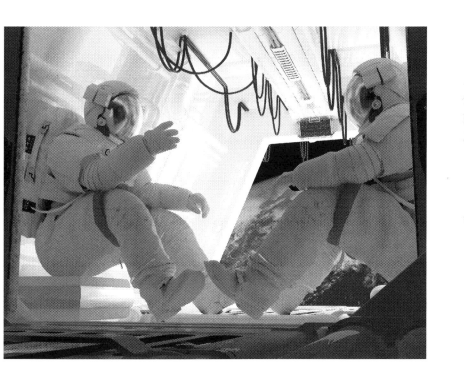

Chapter 21

God's Flame

The Bible is a good source of inspiration, and many books can inspire us, even just paragraphs and sentences in them. Books can move the mountains in us into the sea of our soul, and we can see again how far we can reach. God moves the mountains in us so we can see beyond to the green valleys of nourishment for our souls and so his and our flames of life can burn longer and brighter.

We have been truly blessed with great music and great inspirational speakers. God has already given us much to feed upon. Seek those words to live by; seek those songs that cause the God flame within us to rise above all the troubles and sadness of the world until at last we glow with God's great flame. It will inspire us to rise as nations and people and beliefs that make others want to follow us on our inspirational paths.

Seek those from whom God's flame comes forth when they speak or sing. Worship not them but God, their inspiration. Inspire others by bringing the light of God's flame to them that will change them.

Life changes into a roaring blaze of joy that echoes across the room and out the door down the stairs and goes outside and shouts "Hallelujah" to God, who gave it all to us. We need to ask God to open the windows of heaven and pour out his blessings upon all humanity and nations. Let the miracles begin.

Chapter 22

Welcome the Future

Inspire others with your words or music if you are so blessed. Let those who can design a new world be inspired to do so; let inventions come forth in number and magnitude that stagger the senses.

Become inspired by God's flame of life and contribute to a world that glorifies God, inspires humanity, and makes the world a better place. Let researchers find cures for diseases. Let explorers take the flame to distant worlds as we come in peace. Let us create the future with God at the helm guiding us along a path known only to him. We are limited by the mountain because we can't see over it. We are limited by the forest because we are so close to it we cannot see the trees. We are limited by our egos and confidence and desires to get rich so much that we forget the purpose of our inspiration.

Let our inspiration be to give God praise for what he gives. Let us inspire others to create and invent. They may be in the dark shadows having given up all hope. Restore their hope and let God be praised. Do not give false hope to people because if they fail, they will be worse than before, but look diligently for real abilities and skills that lie dormant in places you never thought of looking into. From hopelessness comes blessings on us all.

Many have given up one inch from success. Others have pushed on until they created something worthwhile for us all. Don't be blinded by false dreams of what you can do to become rich and famous; find God's fire and riches and skills and abilities within. Let them burn so brightly that you see what God wants you to see and how you can achieve it with his help.

Choose to be the carrier of the flame of God. Don't let others extinguish it. Be like the Olympic torchbearer. Light someone else's flame and then another and another until the world glows with God's light and we live in peace, each one helping the other.

It's easy to go along with those who make fun of happy people. We can drink and take drugs and feel good. Why would we bother with God's flame of joy and happiness if it were just imaginary?

Be the one who stands for God's flame; it will light your path and those of others when they come down off their drugs and alcohol and step out of paths that lead to destruction. God's flame still burns bright, and it's still not too late to help others. Though others never see your inner flame, hang onto it, for in the darkest hour, you will need it to see your way. Darkness doesn't exist in that great, everlasting city God has made. Do not hide your light under a basket; do not pretend it isn't there. Let it shine, and let others know they too can find eternal life through God's everlasting flame.

The greatest miracle you can do for yourself is to bathe in the light God gives you and be filled until your cup runs over. Let yourself feel the power of the Holy Spirit; you will be ready for whatever the future holds. Go forward until you find the advanced civilization that has never existed before. God's mighty flame will lead you there.

Chapter 23

A Word or Phrase

Fold back the pages of books where you find words that inspire you. Make them part of your life. Nahum 1:13 loosened the chains that were holding me down. God inspired me to read it over and over. Each time I did, a new word or a new meaning for a word popped out at me. For years, I read it daily. It changed my life. I threw it into the face of the darkness that was holding me down. It offered me continual strength.

We can research words or phrases and find scriptures and books that will free us from bondage and fear. Never have we needed a greater force than God's flame of fire and inspiration. We spend hours watching TV or on the Internet seeking information and never know God's flame exists. We should seek the future with a greater inspiration from God. Our ears and minds are so full of songs and poems and books and movies created by others who have influenced us. Now, we should be inspired, not just influenced, to determine what we need to change in the world and in ourselves for the betterment of all humanity.

Keep looking. Find the words that come the closest to inspiring you and the flame of God. Rise into a new world until you and others see where this great ship called earth is going because somebody forgot to turn on the headlights and at times we seem close to going off a cliff.

Do you find inspiration in what others have written that has changed your life and soul? Perhaps someone gave you the golden words you needed but you were too busy to listen or didn't realize their importance for your life. Perhaps you've been seeking new words to help you find your way. Perhaps it isn't an invention or a cure but a simple word or phrase that will change you forever. Perhaps what you say to others are words that contain love for each other, and that's God's love.

Chapter 24

Just a Reminder

Some people carry crosses, pictures, or other items to remind them of their resolve to change their lives. Such items help them when nobody is around or they feel nobody cares about them.

Can we change the future? Why would we then choose the path of destruction knowing we will extinguish the flame of life in us? Why do we not choose to use our God-given minds to create things that make the world better for ourselves and those without hope? Why place it all upon those who do not deserve to suffer when God has given us the power to overcome what may destroy our children and grandchildren?

Be inspired to live your life in a way that makes you proud. Be inspired and find the inspiration that fuels the mind body and spirit. Light the God flame within. He has given it to you, so you should never let it go out. It will illuminate his path for you. Do not look to humanity to light your inner flame; seek God's light, which is much brighter. You will see him welcoming you with love and open arms.

Write some inspirational words down and carry them with you at all times. Read them daily and incorporate them into your life. The Bible is a great place to find inspiration. It contains timeless words that will echo far into the future.

Chapter 25

Awaken the Great Minds

Awaken ye of great minds. Awaken ye of great inventions. Awaken ye people who know the secret words that inspire. Awaken to a new age. Awaken to a new world. Awaken to a new sunrise where there is no end in sight of God's greatness. Awaken with God's mighty flame of the spirit and know that God has intervened and given to us the greatest gift of recent times. Let peace prevail, and let us be proud as nations seek the love and friendship of one another. Let families and friends rejoice and say, "Hallelujah."

We must be prepared for whatever the future holds. We must promote whatever makes others rich. Our jealousy of others' wealth should not keep us from our future. With God's help, our thoughts may produce something simple yet helpful and wonderful so much that we wondered why it hadn't been invented before.

Let the future come. Be ready for it. God's flame will show us the way. We can manage our lives in all things through the one who strengthens us beyond our fears and imaginations. We can become a civilization greater than any other. We can be the generation that becomes the foundation of all generations to come. Let history look at our generation and say, "Thank you."

What does the future hold for us? What can we wish for that would change our lives for the better? What would we like the future to be? Can we predict our future based on what we see today? Will it be enjoyable or a nightmare? We can imagine it somewhat based on science fiction and things we find on the Internet. Movies show us monsters and creatures that could come about, but we need to focus on the good of humanity, not how fierce people or things can look or act.

Why can't we imagine a God who is without limits and allows us to create an unlimited world for good things to be created? Would we rather float along and see what happens and not ask God? Do we secretly want to destroy all other generations before us and let only the strong survive? What about the smart people? Do they deserve to live? What about the people who cannot protect themselves or even walk? Should we do away with all of those who are disabled and weak? Hopefully not.

Chapter 26

It Doesn't Matter Where You Sit

Do we cheat ourselves out of God in life? Why would we do the very thing that can make our lives better by avoiding God? What would starving people do if we tried to feed them? If they were afraid, they might avoid the food to feel safe. Are we afraid of God? Is our fear of him our greatest enemy? When God reaches out to us, what do we fear? He who made us can touch us anytime he wishes, so how can we avoid God?

We run away from God to avoid him for one reason or another. We may deny he exists to avoid him. Has evolution ever been called upon for help by anyone hanging by one arm from a cliff? Who else can you call upon except God? We often turn to technology, but it can fail us. Our phones can be out of range. Better to have God. No concrete wall can block God. No place is so remote that God cannot reach it. No situation is so hopeless that God cannot fix it.

Do not cheat yourself out of God by denying he exists. You cheat only yourself. Come to him and receive the food he offers you. He feeds the spirit, and that's where we hunger the most. We need to satisfy our souls' hunger above all else.

Imagine seeing a movie twice but in different seats in the theater. The change of perspective doesn't affect the outcome; the movie always ends the same. But life is not like that. You can indeed change life's outcomes. Imagine asking God to change the future for the good of all humanity and he did just that. God is unlimited; he is capable of things you cannot imagine, but you live based on your belief in your limitations.

How can we understand we can live only so long or eat so much or travel just so far in a day or lifetime? Are limits what life is all about? How good can we be? How fast can we go? What can we do nobody else can? To rely on God means we just pray and he does it or makes it possible to happen. How difficult can we make that? A one-second, single-sentence prayer to God can change lives.

Try what you believe to be the thing you do best. Try it over and over until you feel you have a world record for doing that one thing. Become the heavyweight champ of the world. God already assumes you are because he loves you. Ask him in prayer what you want or hope the world will become and see if the world moves in that direction. God gives us life. Nobody or nothing else can give us that day after day.

Chapter 27

Whisper God's Name

Whisper God's name and he will hear you. Shout God's name and he will hear you. Deny he exists or curse him and he will hear you but still love you. His love cannot be erased.

In the life to come, we will receive judgment for what we have done or not done. Look up into the sky at night and he will see you. Look down at the ground as hard as you can and he will see you. No matter what you do, he will see you. Try not saying anything or thinking one thought. He's still there. Try not feeling anything, and he still feels love for you.

God is inescapable; he never leaves us. We belong to him, but too often, we reject him as a father. Since God is so aware of us, he knows our problems. We should hand them to him. We should ask him for a future world beyond anything we could imagine. God is unlimited, but perhaps we put limits on him in our minds and believe he won't listen. We are no longer living in caves or driving horses and buggies. Something changed. Was it because we just got smarter, or did God intervene and make it possible for us to progress?

Let us assume for a moment we have the power to ask him for unlimited things. Would he hear us and grant our requests? God's riches reach out gently and do not go where they aren't welcome. He is still unlimited in his power to help us. What help do we need?

What stops us from asking? If we proceed in the direction of God and believe he can hear us, he will answer our prayers. We need to pray boldly to him for amazing gifts of the future. We must believe, not just assume. Believing goes beyond assuming. We must ask God to do something truly amazing for us.

We need fuel of different types to travel, to live. All fuels come from his creation, even wind and solar power. Oil, coal, and atomic energy are all part of God's earthly creation. He opened ways to mine it or build ways to convert it or make it work for us. Let us assume then that God could or would provide us with a new source of energy.

Let's assume we could utilize gravity as a fuel or invent an antigravity mechanism. Perhaps we could place a little thrust into it and travel wherever we wanted. We could cross international boundaries easily and make friends and go home.

Antigravity could help us relax in saunas and travel to the stars. Since God has no limits, he would be with us wherever we went, wherever we were. He could comfort us, and we might even give him thanks and praise for such a gift.

Chapter 28

It's Happened Before

God could also provide us with genetic restructuring. We'd be able to avoid diseases. We'd be able to become long-distance runners or weightlifters. Sounds impossible, doesn't it? But if it were true, doctors could operate on us using computers even if they were miles away. Maybe we'd be able to operate on ourselves.

We need something to deal with the medical issues we're all subject to. We need God to assist us with creations that are possibly within reach now but may not be available in our lifetime. Pray to God for miracles that change our lives for the better. If he does love us, and he does, he will provide a future beyond our imagination.

If we travel to remote parts of the world, we need protection from the elements. Imagine having a backpack in which we packed a tent that could expand and be hardened by some chemicals that would make it as sturdy as a house. Imagine having in that backpack enough high-energy food to feed us for days. Imagine having something, perhaps a capsule, that could expand even small amounts of water exponentially.

Perhaps such shelters could solve the needs of the homeless. Perhaps such food could feed the hungry everywhere. Perhaps such water enhancers could offer people all the water they needed. God can do many things with our minds to help us create our way out of problems.

Darkness is always a worry, but we have devices that allow us to see in the dark. What if their use was expanded? Night-vision technology could be coupled with technology that would let us know exactly what we are seeing and how to respond to it—friend or foe? No matter where we were, we would be able to recognize our situation and how to respond to it and ask for help as necessary.

God wants us to be safe, and in many situations, we need his help whether it be in times of war, natural disasters, or medical emergencies wherever we are. We can all imagine a future of some kind that is wonderful, and with the help of God, we can all live safely and in peace.

Chapter 29

Is the Answer in a Pill?

We look to the future, but we must learn from the past. We tend to forget the miracles of the Bible or treat them as myths. We cannot duplicate most of the biblical miracles even with our present technology. It is progressing toward things that help us live safer and longer, but it also helps us create more-deadly weapons.

In Exodus 7:10, Aaron's rod turned into a serpent. Imagine having that kind of power that isn't just a magician's trick. In Exodus 7:20, water was turned into blood. If doctors could do that today, many lives would be saved. In Exodus 14:6, the Red Sea parted as Moses held high his staff.

In Joshua 10:12, the sun and moon stood still. How was that possible considering the earth rotates? Scientists have not been able to find a way that could be done, but some believe it could have happened because of the scientific analysis of time itself.

In Daniel 3:19, three men were thrown into a furnace and exited it without even the smell of smoke on them.

Quite likely, these were all miracles, but we need not have such dramatic miracles; we can and do have smaller miracles every day through the power of prayer. God can help us create technology that carries not just across the Red Sea but across galaxies at speeds we haven't even imagined. Scientists are working feverishly night and day on quantum mechanics, but we need to work on God's mechanics—prayer—which doesn't require scientists.

Simply speak to God and ask him for ways to make our world better and more at peace. Some in the world profit from war; we must protect ourselves night and day. Pray that wars do not come. Pray for the future world to come.

In 1 Samuel 17:1–25, David slew Goliath with a simple sling and stone. Imagine the surprise at the end of that event. It was far more surprising than any bowl game or world series game could ever be. Have we changed much since the days of the event that created King David? What would be the result and consequences if we proceeded today? We wish for the outcome of games to go our way, but when we really need God's help, we do not pray. Wishing has no real power. Faith in God has power. Pray to God with faith; do not just pray and wish. What about the wisdom of Solomon, supposedly the wisest man ever? How do we create wisdom? Didn't God bless Solomon?

Chapter 30

Why Does God Open the Door?

Science needs to help us when we need help. We have airbags and all manner of safety devices on cars. Why don't we have safety devices on our personal lives? Imagine having those kinds of devices. Science is trying to alter us through genetics and other methods, but will it be the kind of help we need? Will we rid ourselves of dangerous people?

In time of war, we need professional soldiers unafraid of the enemy. We need to live in peace. Peace requires protection, so we should ask God for that protection.

God can prevent evil things from happening through not only miracles but through technology that warns and protects us from our enemies. In the process of advancing, we have forgotten how we got here. With God's help, lethal diseases have been eradicated. Today, those with AIDs, heart disease, and cancer are living longer. Can we just say science is our God? Right after we solve one problem, another seems to pop up, so how can we call science our God? If science were our God, would we bow down and worship an image we created that symbolized a science God? What would that God look like? Perhaps we bow down more than we think before television sets or the Internet or our cell phones; they all seem to take over our minds, but our minds were made by God.

We spend billions on medications every year. What if we suddenly didn't need them? If we're on medication, we should stay on them to avoid potential danger. I'm not suggesting stopping medication of any kind, but God's healing powers are capable of miracles beyond our limited imaginations.

Our beliefs are what have gone away. We seem to think the less we believe in God, the smarter and more intelligent we are. We believe we don't need his help. But when things go beyond our scientific beliefs, we suddenly become religious. Imagine a great meteor heading toward earth and only God could change its course. Would we pray to God for that miracle? When would we feel it's okay to pray to God? When we or someone we know has an incurable ailment? Would we pray if our car was hanging over the edge of a bridge?

We don't need to assume that devastation is on its way; it's just a matter of time until it gets here. We get older, our genetic makeup breaks down, or we are afflicted by a disease. We're aging faster than we'd like to, but if God could perform a miracle that caused these things to change, would we pray? And would anything change?

Chapter 31

Water into Wine?

Optimism can help people get through tough situations. People who have been imprisoned for years see the light of day and can't believe it's possible. Often, they become so overwhelmed they can't adjust and end up back in prison.

God can help people make transitions through miracles beyond what science can do. Counseling has helped many people as have motivational speakers and coaches, but God can change someone instantly into a survivor or person who is cured of an ailment. God can make others so wealthy and healthy that we wouldn't recognize them.

We don't need to change water into wine. We don't need to miraculously feed five thousand with a few sandwiches a boy may have brought along. We don't need to catch a fish that has in its mouth the exact amount of money that can pay our taxes. We simply need God's help daily. We need order for society and civilization to move forward; we need God's wisdom and invention. We need to pray to God to provide us with what we need whether it's food or health. To wonder how God will do something miraculous is to deny God ever helped us. Some people might say "It would have happened with or without God." Without understanding God's power over everything, we cannot say that.

When we pray, we use words outside the realm of learning, evolution, and science. Science needs God, so pray for science to believe in God more so scientists might rejoice at the wonders he or she performs. God allows for the unknown but not if he is placed in the Santa Claus box until Christmas or Easter where the unknown aspect of God dwells and is left to die there. No wonder people say God is dead. He is dead to them. Unknowns are not allowed in science if they pertain to God. "Show me God and I'll believe," they might say. You might ask if they couldn't find an explanation to make him go away. If science would incorporate God into its devices, discoveries, and inventions, we might move even faster down the corridor of progress.

Chapter 32

Can We Awaken Science?

Science makes itself a decision maker in the world of religion. Science declares something, so it must be true. But much of science is rewritten in just a few years. Scientists will step out and boldly say, "God doesn't exist," but they have no proof. There is no body to examine, nor is there any empirical evidence God doesn't exist. There is no test to be done, so we rely on evidence provided by people who quite likely don't believe in God to prove God doesn't exist. I respect their beliefs, but why place it as gospel before everyone? Let others decide if God exists or not.

Nothing has changed in history, and the Bible provides evidence, so why is that not a consideration when many biblical events can be empirically proven? We seek information on the pyramids as if they were mystically powerful, but we don't even know for sure how they were built. Reckless conclusions based on theory are not proof. God, however, exists in religions around the world, and many pray to him every day. Are millions of people wrong?

Science just cannot make God go away. We should pray to God regardless of scientific theories. Let science lead us into new inventions and devices that make life better and safer. Let that be the job of science based on logic and physics, which God created. Let unbelievers remain unbelievers until they pray and find out

God hears their prayers as well. "If God exists, why doesn't he show himself?" they ask. They somehow know he doesn't exist because they say he doesn't exist. But he's there when the sun rises and sets. He's been there since the beginning, and he will be there forever. He isn't planning on leaving.

Our minds function through time, space, and matter to solve equations far beyond our experience in classrooms. Minds speak to God and ideas within us. Are we using ESP? The amazing thing is that many people believe prayer is simply asking for simple things such as food and water. They don't realize God performs miracles as well. The Lord's Prayer starts with a recognition of God's holy name. We don't know what a holy God is, but we recognize he is holy. We are not holy for the most part.

"Give us this day our daily bread." Symbolic I believe of what God gives us when we pray. "Give us bread," we say because in that day, bread was all people needed along with water or wine. Occasionally, they ate fish and honey. They could have said, "Give us a magic sword to defeat all our enemies," but the prayer says bread. We have plenty of bread today, so it's obvious we've received it; why do we still ask for it? What if we say, "Give us the things we need beyond our bread"? Maybe we should ask God to give something totally different. Perhaps we need new inventions or cures. He knows our needs before we ask. We are intelligent beings, but we will need things from him as long as we live.

Keep an open mind and an open line to God, and don't hesitate to ask him for what's most important in your life whether a career or healing or strength. Perhaps you want to be person who helps others in any number of ways. The God door is open, so ask and see if he answers. You will very likely change your future in some way or other because most likely you will receive an answer.

It doesn't matter if we don't have a way to measure faith and miracles and prayers; what matters is the outcome. Read the Bible to discover who God is and who we are in his sight. Give him the chance to prove himself to you through miracles.

The prayer of a righteous man can be very effective (James 5:16). If we just keep doing the same thing and nothing changes, we can blame only ourselves.

Science has given us much, and religion has changed the world as well. A great chasm exists between scientific reasoning and faith in God. The marriage of science and religion must begin, for together with God's many miracles, we can conquer space and perhaps even time. Let us look to both for the hope of humanity. Let us look to God first to intercede and bring about great changes in a future we all can share. Assume God is present in every lab and place of research, and pray for discovery and invention for us to find our daily bread or computer data or cell phone calls or medical hospitals and stores where we buy ridiculous toys and gadgets and medications.

We aren't evil because we have toys; we are needful of God, and that makes us weak and in danger of losing everything unless we seek him. Wishing for so many things to be given to us, we forget to ask God in prayer. Wishing for things that God does not want us to have may be difficult to understand, but in time, we will see why he didn't give it to us. We must be patient.

What else can we expect in the future? What miraculous things can God give us? Let our minds abound with creative thoughts and hopes of a new world, a world in which the awakening of humanity occurs and we say thank you to God in a holy way recognizing his almighty power and receiving his love. Let us reason together and produce the most magnificent creations God will allow. With God's help, science fiction will become a thing of the past. We will live in a world where peace prevails and we all receive our daily bread. What will be your daily bread? What will you ask God to do?

Let us imagine that our creative spirits and minds have no limits. Because God is unlimited, so are we. Perhaps we place limits on ourselves. After all, we are flawed, so why shouldn't we be able create as our creator can? Why shouldn't we be able to do the unthinkable and create the science fiction that could be prophecy? Perhaps there is no such thing as science fiction, only limitations we place on ourselves. Let us look at what we used to consider the impossible.

Time travel seems so distant that we don't consider it possible, but scientists are researching it. Imagine being able to go back in time and seeing your relatives or friends or even your younger self. You might be surprised at who you once were. You might realize your younger self could do things but you never knew that. You might want to help your earlier self be more successful, but the laws of the universe might prohibit that from happening.

Imagine being able to travel into the future and seeing the way the world really is going to be. Would you really want to see that? You might be surprised to see traffic on highways stacked on different levels flowing freely. The wonders of the future have not been revealed, yet we grow ever closer to our need for its technology. We need God's help to catch up with our needs.

If we could see into the future, say one hundred years from now, we might see many devices that entertain us. Perhaps long before that hundred years, inventions, devices, and techniques might amaze us. We might see movies that we generate with actors from the past playing roles in new movies. We could adjust movies to suit ourselves with people we can create fictionally and create games that satisfy us or create music sung by us in place of the singer. No need for real people when we could synthesize our own voices into movies and change tones and do whatever we want in the movie. We would become actors, directors, and producers of our personal movies.

Holographic imagery might become common in the future; we could visit people anywhere without moving an inch. We could take vacations anywhere without flying or driving. We could be visited by reproductions of famous singers or actors or athletes. We could become influential not by tweeting but transporting ourselves holographically. We could even create holographic mansions for ourselves anywhere we wanted. We could transport ourselves for checkups or tests rather than waiting for hours at a doctor's office. Doctors across the country could consult about our conditions.

They might even consult with robots and computers, which might ultimately replace doctors and help us in so many other ways.

People on the verge of dying might regularly be cryogenically frozen until the technology or medical care they need becomes reality. Many things can be created in our hungry and thirsty world, including that water enhancer and high-energy foods I mentioned.

Imagine what the future holds for us.

Chapter 33

Could There Be Another You?

Could it be possible for us to shape our bodies by getting in molds of the bodies we want? Could we clone ourselves? Could we transplant our brains into another body, a healthier body, as we do other organs?

We have yet to take advantage of the ocean; it is a marvelous resource. We could convert seawater to fresh water and farm fish if we wanted to live on or under the oceans. We could create vast cities underground. We already have great capabilities; what can God give us to complete the process? Perhaps prayer can provide answers in the form of ideas and technology and knowledge.

Speaking in the future may be done by ESP or thought transmission. Though the world is filled with many languages, thought transmitters could do the translations we require and transmit our thoughts and words to others even across great distances. This might be helpful to scientists engaged in the same research but separated by many miles. Thoughts could be sent to giant computers and the information analyzed and compared to other scientific data; new information could come forth quickly.

Chapter 34

Are We Really at Peace?

Social problems need be solved because we need to live in peace. Prisons have almost proven they cannot change people. Perhaps a new type of prison would be one in which people would learn the skills they need to become productive workers once they are back in society. The skills needed will change in time, but many people in prison are intelligent and could learn them for their own and society's benefit.

Imprisonment suppresses minds as well as people; perhaps we can reprogram minds and help them focus on prosperity rather than crime. People can be cruel, but we need great minds to solve great problems and moral issues.

Schools can utilize methods to analyze the geniuses in the classroom or determine if all the students are geniuses in different ways. We've herded students through classrooms regardless of what knowledge would actually benefit them individually. Robots might prove to be wonderful teachers much more capable of dealing with individual students' educational needs. Imagine students completing high school in two years or college in six months. Medical school in a year. We could end up with doctors, lawyers, and engineers who are twelve years old.

We can only imagine the future. If we could instantly make

changes in it, what would they be? With God's help, we can create a future beyond our imagination. The future is real, and so are we. So is God, and with his help and guidance, we will proceed in wisdom, not chaos. We don't need a world of everyone for himself or herself. No more Wild Wests in which only the quickest guns survived. We want everyone to be a part of the future. Let no mind be left behind. Let no one fall through the cracks of technology. Let those who have abilities to contribute do so.

Let us find the greatest inventors, artists, designers, and people with minds that can be opened and utilized for the good of all. Let us produce leaders who understand the plight of the poor, the elderly, and the sick. Let the wounded be healed and the sick recover.

We need the brightest of minds and the best of prayers to come forth. When Peter saw Jesus walking on the water in Matthew 14:29–31, he walked a few steps toward him before his fear made him sink. Jesus helped him, and Peter survived. We must walk in faith to God, whose help we will need in the future. We must find those who can help us rise from our present state and walk tall and confidently above the problems of the world.

Have we created our own ashes? Have we made our own world one in which we must rise again before we can move forward? Are we now so complacent that we can no longer move forward? Do we need God to help us rise? May God help us.

Chapter 35

Gifts of God

Our greatest accomplishments may lie in genetic engineering. Our genes may carry secrets we simply cannot see. Science looks to genes for illnesses. Let us look further into our genetic pool and find what's there for us and the unborn. We are made by God; his seed is in us all. Let us inspire, motivate, and encourage one another. Let us leave no stone unturned in our quest to find what God wants us to have. God's wish is that we have life and have it abundantly. Let us praise him for that.

Adam and Eve ate of the tree of knowledge. Where is that knowledge? Is it truly knowledge? Would God place a less-than-mighty tree in the Garden of Eden? That tree of knowledge was taken by God, but within all of us lies genetic knowledge because of that first bite of the fruit. What if God decided to bring back that tree of knowledge and we somehow could eat of it? Are we capable of eating it after all this time? Are we capable of handling that much knowledge?

God is in the knowledge business and need not bring back the tree, but he can open our minds and allow us the chance to proceed with his help. We must first humble ourselves and acknowledge God as all powerful and holy. We must place him above all other gods. We must realize his greatness and ask him for the keys to the future.

We can advance in God in ways we cannot imagine. Through God, we are often healed and blessed. In the process of daily living, we may be calling upon him a thousand times and not know it. He hears our cries and inner pain yelling out daily, and through his love, we survive and our children have hope. Take away the hope of God and we are lost in mind and body. It would be as if the sun went dark and the earth became dark and cold. With God's light and that of the sun, we survive and live.

Survival is our first goal, but moving forward is important too. Let us not try the patience of a loving God. Let us not anger the greatest asset we have. Let us not suppose we can go it alone when the chances of survival without him would be very small. The reality is that with him we can do all things and be victorious. As we glorify him, let our future begin anew and let hope reign in us forever.

Chapter 36

Let It Shine

Let It Shine

Let God's light shine within you
Let it Glow and Grow until it radiates outward
Let it Glow in your face and let your entire body shine
Let it shine within the deep canyons of your soul
Let it shine through your eyes
Let it shine until the whole world can see it in you
     Let God's light so shine that God's love radiates from within you
Let it shine until the darkness surrenders before its light
 Let your light so shine that the darkness breaks
Let it shine like a bright star on a clear night sky
 Let it shine without end into the blackness
 Let it shine into the face of all that is evil
  Let it shine until you can see the face of God through the darkness
     Let it shine and let pain flee before it
   Let it shine until loneliness and emptiness fall into the abyss
   Let it shine and penetrate every crack and crevice of hell and evil
  Let it shine as God destroys hell and then rebuilds a new world
Let it shine into the hope of that new world where the ashes of hell lie

Let it shine and let the ashes of hell become God's garden of hope
and love
Let it shine until God makes it explode into a new world of life,
love, and beauty
Let it shine upon a new world where beauty is beyond description
Let it shine in peace and joy overwhelming
Let it shine now and forever in us

—Kenneth Foley

Chapter 37

Where Are the Great Minds?

According to the Bible, Paul was well educated as a Roman, but that wasn't counted against him as he wrote several books of the New Testament. Being intelligent doesn't mean not believing in God. Many intelligent people are quite religious and are even devoted to serving God. Even Einstein believed in God.

Where then are the great minds? Are they in college classrooms? Are they in laboratories doing medical research? Are they doctors or lawyers or politicians? Perhaps they are writing books or counseling others. It seems we have very little knowledge of who is intelligent.

Common sense is intelligence; people often repair or devise things just for amusement. Many intelligent people spend hours playing games on the Internet. People with wisdom may seek God and try to define matters for us. Where then are the intelligent people who will take us into the future? All in Silicon Valley making large sums of money but doing very little to help humanity solve its problems? Are they creating technology that could help us?

Where are those who challenge the minds of our children and help us create a generation of geniuses to help us? How many geniuses does it take to support a hundred unemployed people or people on welfare who never plan on working? How many geniuses can teach a hundred people to utilize their God-given skills? Where can we look for creative geniuses? Are there many kinds of geniuses who can create in different ways? Where are those gifted geniuses who can teach children and grown-ups alike?

Perhaps the greatest singers never sang because they never realized they had that talent. It could be the same with guitarists and drummers. How can we define a genius just in the music field alone?

Can we look under every rock so to speak to discover those with talent and genius? What about imagination? Can we find those who can imagine while others create? Have we failed many of our people because we didn't want to disturb anyone? What does race, age, height, or weight matter? Are we unable to discover people who can create because we have no way to discover who they are?

What if we had Olympic games of the mind? Competition has a way of bringing out the best in us. What events could people compete in? That could be a way of discovering and uncovering our best minds, those that can handle math, engineering, and problem solving of all types. We might be able to measure the unique brain waves of geniuses. Maybe we could find people who can discover why some people want to kill others or spend their lives in prison.

We must leave it with the geniuses of the future to figure out such matters. We cannot, however, leave God out of the equation. We alone cannot solve every problem.

Chapter 38

Beneath the Waterfall with Only a Cup

Suppose we already have the greatest skill maker helping us but don't recognize it. No competition took place to find a warrior to face Goliath; David rose to the occasion. The prophet Samuel sought out Jesse, a shepherd, who had several sons. Samuel looked at each son and said he was not the one. Until David, a mere boy, walked into the room.

We have not because we ask not. If we sought God for prophets and wise people who could speak to God or just hear God, would we do so? If we had a Samuel to stand between us and tomorrow's problems, would we seek him? If we had the same God to go to, could we find answers for today's problems?

Would our perfect conception of knowledge outweigh one of God's people? Do we need more of God's chosen ones to come forth? Have we grown into such wise people that we don't need anyone but ourselves? Did we create the messes in the world today by ourselves?

Who would think an eagle could soar through the sky and swoop down on a bear cub or fox or other animal bigger than itself? Who can imagine the small things of the world overcoming the great things? How can we find the shepherd boys and girls today who will lead us in the future? Who can sing songs and give God praise as David did? Who will lead our world as our problems become more complex? Only a God who is greater than the most complex of problems can solve the equations of today and tomorrow.

We will advance only on the day we forgive each other and look to a mighty God. On that day, we will be in sync with the universe and understand what he has given us. We will accept the fact that he is far greater than we can imagine.

The creator is greater than the created. The creator can solve our problems. Is the air around us so lacking in the oxygen of prayer that we cannot see we're in our hour of need and lack those who can pray on behalf of us all? Can we not see the yoke upon us that makes it impossible for us to solve our social, political, and religious problems? Can we not see that God has created a way out of bondage that leads us to knowledge and freedom?

Can we not see that the geniuses are in the boys or girls within us whom nobody recognizes because there is no Samuel to point to the geniuses in us? Can we see that our inner children humble themselves before God and allow God through faith to slay the giant problems we have and produce the greatest age we have ever seen? Creator and created would be in tune with one another and working together until they were joined in that utopian world of the future.

Chapter 39

Why Would God Teach Us New Ideas?

Imagine a necklace bright with gems. Imagine each gem as an idea or problem solver. Imagine God lighting those gems one at a time during our lives and giving us the answers and knowledge we need. That is simplifying the way God works. We don't even need such necklaces; we need to pray to God, who sees our prayers like diamonds in the sky reaching out to him. He welcomes our prayers with joy and gives us gifts. They may be hidden from us for a long time, but they are his to give; he gives them to us all and not just us when we pray. That doesn't make us perfect, just unbelievably happy and at peace with him and all he has made as we see the world change into a better place.

Bits of information come to us every day like gems on a necklace. They constitute a waterfall of information, and we stand under it with just a cup. We need buckets to collect enough of that information to create the utopian world we desire. The fruit is falling off the tree, so to speak, as we stand looking at the tree.

Reap God's harvest through prayer and seeking God. He will not disappoint you. Patience is part of the gathering of God's fruit; it's necessary to sift through what God gives us until we find the pieces that fit. God will give us understanding of his gifts if we pray for that understanding.

We don't need geniuses to change the world; prayer surpasses all forms of genius. We stand in awe of an intelligent God who has knowledge and wisdom that surpasses all understanding. We should be humbled by God's greatness yet amazed that he does not look down on us in a way that makes us feel smaller. He wants us not to fail. He listens to our prayers and answers them in ways that change our lives and make us truly alive.

His love for us may be the most difficult thing we will ever try to understand. It's in the stars and the seas and the flowers. His love is in the eyes of a child and in the voice of a parent. He is there for us day and night. He waits for us to answer his love with thanksgiving and praise. He waits for us to adore and worship him. He waits for our prayers that ask him for miracles that awaken us to a new and wonderful world where we will all live in peace and prosperity.

Chapter 40

A God of Surprises

Who then is the hero in the story of David and Goliath? Was it David, who killed the giant, or was it Samuel, who saw the boy and knew God had chosen him not only to slay the giant but also to be the king? Was it God, who taught David during the hours he spent tending sheep to use the sling? It seems God was preparing David to become king, not just Goliath's slayer.

What is God teaching you? What is God preparing in your life for you? Are you to become a great leader? Are you to slay a giant? Most people would say that if God was teaching them something, they didn't know what that was.

Look between the lines. What you are now doing involves something else, but God is preparing you or has prepared you for something. If David had denied his ability, he would never have slain that giant or never been heard from. David knew the sling was a weapon that could kill a giant, but he still relied on God, and so should you.

If you deny what God has planned for your life, you won't accomplish it. We are most happy when we allow ourselves to give in and follow the plan God has for us no matter the genius we have. Utopia is not built on denials but on acceptances brick by brick. Accept what God wants you to do today and do it. Seek out what

God wants you to do and find a utopian feeling only God can give. You need not be a hero, just a person doing what God prepared you to do long ago when you were younger and even today. He has taught you something, and it's your job to find if you are good with a sling, or if you can sing, or if you can do any number of things that glorify God.

Where is the genius in you? Seek the answer and find your place before God. He has undoubtedly sent someone to tell you what you need to do. If you will graciously accept God's gift of intelligence, you'll be blessed of God. Why not accept the fact that God can help you and let the miracle in you awaken? Let the miracle that the world is waiting for come out and bless others. Put yourself in God's hands and honor him with your skill, service, or genius.

Where are the great and mighty men and women? Where are those who serve God as missionaries and teachers? Where are those who pray to God night and day and praise and honor his name? Only God knows who and where they are. Perhaps they are elderly women struggling on meager pensions but still donating to missions. Maybe they're a young married couple not sure of their future but are committed to God.

Who prays for the unfortunate? Who prays for children in danger of any type? Who prays for the sick and dying of any age? Why bother to pray? Does God hear our prayers?

Taste and see that he is good. Pray and watch what he does. He hears your prayers and acts in a way that will be for your good and the good of all humanity.

Let those who pray begin to pray more and with greater faith. Let those who invent, or design, or solve problems continue to do so with fervor. Let the peacemakers prevail so all will live in peace and prosperity. May all the world rejoice and celebrate God's goodness.

Let us find what is holy in ourselves and bring it to the surface. Let us bring it to the altar and place it before God. Let us seek holiness in all God's creation. Let God's light shine on our faces, and let us create a new, beautiful world.

Chapter 41

Christmas Morning

Our prayers will help us discover cures for our diseases. Reach deep into your mind and soul and pray for those who study and care for others. Let devices come forth in abundance as never before to enhance our ability to overcome sickness.

Let creative geniuses come forth in great multitudes and find new music that glorifies God. Let logic cease to exist in the minds of unbelievers, and let them see with new eyes and hear with new ears that God is there for them to pray to. Let them be filled with God's Spirit of love and thanksgiving as a new life has begun.

If God will give it to us, we should use it. If God will show it to us no matter how obscure and unbelievable, may we find a use for it. What God gives, let all of us receive. Let God multiply the devices and inventions he gives as he multiplied the loaves and fishes for the multitude. Let us be blessed more than Christmas morning gives joy and happiness. Let the surprises of discovery come from places unknown to us. In laboratories across the world, let great discoveries be made. In the backyards and basements, let new ideas come forth.

The Bible is filled with discovery. Its language spoken long ago brings forth new fruit and new meaning every day for those who read it. Treasures lie hidden in its pages for those who study it. Read it without knowing, and let it teach you. The Bible is a great and mighty teacher and has taught many things to many great people.

The greatest of truths is that God loves us. Who would love a people who have rebelled and said God doesn't exist? Who would forgive us for believing he doesn't exist when the very hairs of our heads are known to him?

Chapter 42

What about Aliens?

No order comes from chaos. From an explosion comes death and destruction. From that which mutates comes mutation. We are not mutants but God's intelligent beings placed in an obscure world.

Distant people in distant worlds may look different from us; if they are zebras, they will look like zebras. If they are birds, they will behave accordingly. No matter what peoples or plants or resources are out there in space, may we benefit from them and let God be praised. If we bring back some unknown disease, we will call on God to stop its spread as he has done so often in the past, and he will hear us. Let us pray for a miracle of healing that will touch the unknown diseases of the future.

Great and mighty crops can come forth and feed millions of people. The harvest has been on hold too long. We have the technology to grow many things. Pray that God will intervene and allow his people to be fed food that is healthy and blessed with nutrients that heal our bodies and minds.

Let the darkness flee as we develop new ways to light our paths. Whether it be personal guidance systems that allow us to see in the darkest caves or lights that shine as bright as the noonday sun. Let our minds see plainly as we discover new ways to learn about others in distant lands, and through social networking, let barriers fall and friendships rise. Let us cease from wars and find new friendships of nations. May each contribute one to another not in financial competition but in sharing the needs and burdens of one another.

Let generations to come rejoice that we made the way with God's help, and let doors be opened and roads and bridges cross oceans and travel under the seas. Hope and pray that technology will not hide from us. May we flourish because we prayed and God heard us and opened the windows of heaven and it rained ideas and gifts of the spirit we never knew were possible.

Let all the earth rejoice. Let humanity profit from God's blessings. May we live in a world free of disease and filled with peace. Let people rejoice and be blessed and created anew. Let the Holy Spirit direct our lives. Let him teach us love and peace and true happiness. Let our genius come forth hand in hand with God. Let the lonely be lonely no more, let those who grieve over lost loved ones find solace in new hope. Let those who believed they would not live be healed of their ailments. And let God be praised.

We seek a solution in the sky. We seek the answers on other planets as we marvel at what God has done in the heavens. We are bombarded with God's beauty evident in his lavish playground with artistic creations that cover millions of years of time that are but a blink of the eye in his time.

Chapter 43

Distant Traveler

To a Distant Traveler

Venture out O distant traveler
travel to distant planets far
travel to moons and galaxies far
travel to distant nebulae and stars
Venture out traveler
Do not be afraid
God who made you
all you see he has also made
Venture out traveler
destinations still unknown
for there are planets galore you must explore
distance may not matter anymore
Venture out traveler
See the wonders made by God
No need to understand as you go
See the beginning of it all as you travel far beyond
Venture out traveler
Beyond images of silver and gold
Into blood red markings

has someone been here before?
This is but the beginning a venture far beyond
What is here? What is there?
What could that shadow be?
Are there shadows in the dawn?
Are they things that are to be?
Made to travel through the stars
your eyes have but to see
beyond Jupiter and Mars
wonders on the horizon
whatever can they be?
Do not fear?
God is near he meant for you to see
The colors forms and beauty
they are near they are far
You hope to capture them in a jar
The same thing he used to make both you and me
This is your place in history this is your destiny
Your eyes can see what else is there
Wonders on horizons whatever can they be?
Venture out traveler
Look out upon ancient rivers and rocks
Do not question they exist
as though they could speak or talk
Touch and feel soil in your hand
Is this the beginning?
is this the promised land?
See and smell its contents
Feel it in your hand
Has this been but a dream?
Did you travel to a star?
Someday you may remember
As you look unto the sky
Ask yourself questions but do not wonder why

Sleep upon immortal thoughts
For you have gone where only God
Has been before
Have others traveled there before?
Sleep upon those immortal thoughts
Someday you may ask and see
The God who made it all
made earth from sea to shining sea
For all mankind to live and see

—Kenneth Foley

Chapter 44

A World beyond Belief

Fill the earth ye Holy Spirit of God. Fill the earth to its very core. As we seek new forms of energy. Fill the earth from the north to the south poles as we seek new sources of food and hidden treasures. Fill the heavens completely, and let it fall for we are most vulnerable of all.

Fill all the earth, Holy Spirit, all around our equator and around the world as we seek peace and friendship as we, one body, rise in praise of a mighty God and at last acknowledge him because no other greatness can reach out and touch the stars. The intelligent creator that made all things under his feet and placed them under ours.

May we enter a great period when peace will prevail and we await the coming to earth of God himself from heaven. We will rejoice and sing and dance, and he will show his face to us for the first time as we embrace his holy presence.

May the sweet taste of God's presence fill the earth and show us a new world filled with things we never imagined. Let God show us the magical and beautiful city from heaven as we rebuild the earth.

Let him show us in his hand the dust that the stars are made of and the light that shines from them. May we learn at his feet why things came to pass in this world and why we stumbled at fought wars and many died.

May those who were dead rise from graves and seas. May they stand before us as we weep at their coming. May we see those we have missed so greatly for so long. May they be as new, and may their faces shine with the presence of God.

May we live in that new world after all things have passed away and the presence of God takes the place of all our needing to know. We will worship him around his throne in music and song and dance and praise.

Let darkness not come near the earth; his light will suffice for all to see. It will shine through us and heal our ailments as he hears our cries and wipes away our tears. It is said the lion will lie with the lamb. Let the evil ones flee before his presence. Let darkness find its deepest hole and disappear. Let the land be free of shadows and thirst; all will be filled from rivers of living waters, and his light shall shine forever as we live forever.

He who comes forth shall sing to us. God himself shall descend from heaven with a shout. Every ear shall hear, and every knee shall bow. Victory over death, sickness, poverty, and pain shall come that day. The doors of prisons and hospitals will open; the sick will be healed and the lame will walk. There shall be a brightness in all the earth for God himself has come.

It is in this hope that we believe and look to God. Each of us has his or her belief, and until that great morning when God does come, let us labor and look up. Let us not seek the darkest corners of the universe for things we can only hope will bring us blessed gifts. Let us look to God to direct our paths not in anger and hate but in love. We need to look always to God to light the true, safe path to him.

Until that day when we all rejoice, may God richly bless us all. We will see him face to face that day; let us not be afraid or ashamed. Let us make God proud of us in all we do and seek him until then. We must continue in prayer and praise night and day. May there be an awakening within us as we rise from what could have been our ashes. Let a new world beyond our genius minds come forth into a miracle where we awaken anew the spirit of God within and we rejoice at his presence.

May we find the real secret of the future in God's holy presence and receive his blessings forevermore. May an awakening of miracles occur in us, and may we rejoice in the hope of a new world in which God is with us always. He will show us the path that leads us into the future, and we will sing his praises forever.

Begin to pray for the miracle awakening of all humanity to find the peace of God through prayer. Find the joy of knowing he hears you as you see your prayers answered. May it lead you to a path of hope for a better world. Together with technology and the discovery of a new world with God as our guide the future of humanity awaits.

Conclusion

My purpose for this book was to praise and thank God for the miracles he has done in my life, to make you feel his richness, and to let you know you can pray to God and be heard. His miracles know no limits, I believe. I encourage you to pray and find the power in prayer. Prayer may seem like an odd request in this day, but try it and see for yourself it works.

My hope is to inspire and motivate you to attain confidence in yourself and believe in God and the ultimate power he has. I pray that somehow you will believe in a power beyond dimensions and space and time, beyond the limits of our earthly minds. I hope you will pray more often than ever for yourself, for the world, and for humanity's future.

Pray that technology will increase greatly and bless us all. Pray that peace and healing will take place around the world and that cures for diseases will be discovered. The need may be greater than we think.

We can climb higher as a people knowing we don't need to look down to see how far we have come. Keep looking upward as far as you can see. Believe we may someday reach the stars.

Let us pray to God with a deep desire to be heard. May our faith be increased as we see the results of praying. God does answer prayer in ways that can confound the mind, but then, we realize God had heard our prayers.

I hope you will benefit from the smallest phrase of encouragement in this book. Do not give up on yourself or God helping you. Be awakened to God throughout your day and even into the darkness of night. It may involve weeping and crying to God from the depths of your soul, but know you are not the first or the last who has wept before God.

We as humans get hurt and sometimes badly; that's when we need God's miracles. Whether it is physical or emotional pain, it hurts, and God knows it. Before that day, let us get to know the God who made us all and believe he who made us can and will help us to overcome the pain whatever form it takes.

It is not my intention to doubt anyone of any religion that believes the Second Coming of Christ is near. The Bible says no man knows the hour when he shall come. To assume we know he is coming is to assume we know his mind. A day can be a thousand years with God; a thousand years can be a day.

I believe God can come at any time. I think God is allowing us to do things we never imagined. We seem to be headed for a great period of technological breakthroughs. If we will indeed be blessed with great inventions and technology, let us ask God for help to use them wisely. Let's be prepared for the ride. Let us allow God to give us the blessings he wants us to have before he comes.

We are quite sure the universe and its galaxies are very old. God has been creating them for a very long time, and our lives are very short. We are not gods by ourselves, but we can do godlike things such as flying and traveling through space. That's because we are his creation and he wants us to soar upward into the heavens if nothing more than to see his work and bow before him.

Because God is evidently so intelligent and powerful, he can do things on our behalf if he so chooses; we must respect him. I believe he will do anything he chooses. I believe that he has allowed us to progress as far as we have for a reason and that he has opened the heavens to us to explore. He may even allow us to travel to distant planets, moons, and stars. We may discover that we are alone among the stars, or we may find other species also made by God. Only the future will tell, and that may be soon.

Prayer is a powerful force not only biblically but also personally. I suggest throughout the book that we pray to God for many things; the list is endless. I pray you will be elevated in your spirit with God's spirit of joy. I hope that through prayer, you will give God a chance to make a new world for the benefit of us all. I wish for you to achieve more in your own life well beyond your expectations and beliefs.

If this book has offended anyone, I apologize. The miracles I have experienced have made me believe in the power of God-given miracles. I hope you will find miracles in your life as well. Miracles that not only can and will save your life but also take you on a walk with God that makes him your best friend and father.

Our miracle awakening awaits us. It's up to us to seek God's help to achieve it and pass through the door ahead of us. We can see the future only dimly; is it an iceberg or a door to the future? If the door is slightly open, let us boldly go through it. What lies beyond is anyone's imagination. Let us pray that we will be ready for whatever future God gives us.

Thank you for reading this book. Please pass it along to anyone you feel it might help. I hope you will read my book *One More Miracle* as well. May both books bless you in many ways.

May God richly bless you, and may you experience many miracles starting today.

Printed in the United States
By Bookmasters